NATURE'S POWER

Written by Patricia K. Kummer

STECK-VAUGHN
ELEMENTARY · SECONDARY · ADULT · LIBRARY

A Harcourt Classroom Education Company

www.steck-vaughn.com

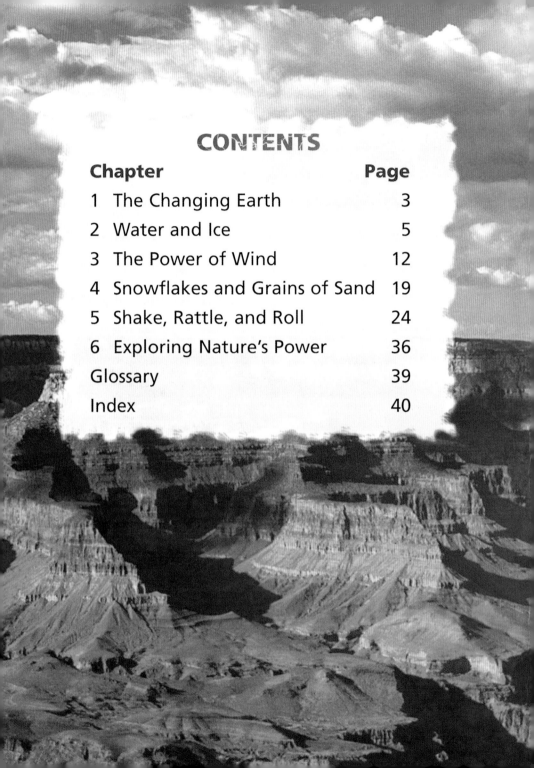

CONTENTS

Chapter 1

The Changing Earth

Our Earth is millions of years old. It is always beautiful, and it is always changing. Sometimes a change happens suddenly. For example, tornadoes often pull trees out of the ground in just seconds. At other times a change can hardly be noticed. Water flowing in a stream loosens pebbles and small bits of soil. Over hundreds of years, the stream slowly becomes a river.

Nature's forces cause many of the changes around us. At times the forces are very powerful. At other times they are gentle. Sometimes nature's forces destroy cities and homes. Sometimes they create beautiful landforms. Nature is an awesome thing!

Sometimes a force of nature acts alone. A light rain may fall for days. The result can be a roaring flood. Nature's forces also act together. Water and cold temperatures can result in icy streets and broken power lines.

Wind and water are forces of nature. So are temperature and gravity. Let's take a look at nature's forces and what they can do.

Wind, water, and temperature have acted alone and together to shape these rock cliffs.

Chapter 2

Water and Ice

People have always needed water. Without water to drink, we would die. We use water for bathing, washing, and cooking. We need rain to grow our food. We also have fun with water. People all over the world enjoy swimming, boating, fishing, and diving. Have you ever watched the waves roll in on a beach? We also like to just sit and look at water.

We need water, and we enjoy it. But water can be very dangerous. It is one of nature's most powerful forces. A driving rain can destroy crops during a thunderstorm. Floods can ruin farmlands, homes, roads, and neighborhoods.

A hard rain can hurt plants.

5

What causes floods? Too much rain can cause rivers to overflow. So can ice and snow that melt too quickly. In 1998 more than 3000 people in China lost their life because rivers flooded the land.

Dams are built on rivers to hold back water. These dams can break and cause floods. That happened in 1889 in Johnstown, Pennsylvania. Most of the city was swept away by a wall of rushing water 30 feet (9 meters) high.

Flash flooding is very quick flooding. It can happen when a slow-moving thunderstorm stays in one place. It also happens when two or more storms travel across the same area.

A flood can wipe out a whole town.

A tsunami's waves can form a deadly wall of water.

A **tsunami** (tsoo NAH mee) is another example of water's great power. The word *tsunami* is a Japanese word that means "harbor wave." A tsunami is actually a group of waves that race across an ocean. The waves are caused by an earthquake or a volcano at the bottom of the ocean.

Tsunamis travel as fast as 600 miles (966 kilometers) per hour. When the waves get close to land, they slow down. Then they catch up with one another and form one huge wave. This wall of water can be as tall as a 20-story building!

The wreckage left behind by a 1994 tsunami in Japan

Lots of water moving very fast can change our lives instantly. In 1946 an earthquake took place under the Pacific Ocean, near Alaska. It started a tsunami. Traveling at 460 miles (741 kilometers) per hour, the tsunami reached Hawaii in only 5 hours. Giant waves crashed onto the land, destroying homes and killing 159 people.

Not all of nature's forces move quickly. Some work slowly over many years. A **glacier** is a thick layer of packed snow and ice. It moves only inches a day. Glaciers slowly carve the land just as a sculptor carves stone. Many are beautiful to look at.

Glaciers form where it is too cold for snow to melt. Each year more snow packs down and turns into ice. The weight of the ice causes it to move downhill.

Many glaciers have names. This one is called Exit Glacier.

More than 10,000 years ago, glaciers covered about $\frac{1}{3}$ of Earth. These glaciers cut valleys in mountains and formed the inlets on the coast of Norway. The glaciers also scooped up rocks from one place and left them in another, creating mountains and more valleys. We call this period of time the Ice Age.

Glaciers left behind soil that is now rich farmland. The moving ice dug large holes, too. When the glaciers melted, the water filled the holes and formed lakes. The Great Lakes in North America were created by glaciers that melted.

Today glaciers hold more than half of the fresh water on Earth. If all the glaciers melted at once, the oceans would rise more than 180 feet (55 meters). Much of the land would be flooded. Luckily, glaciers melt slowly. The water from a glacier flows into rivers and underground streams. It becomes part of the area's drinking water. When people of that area have a glass of water, they are drinking a melted glacier!

Glaciers can be found in several parts of the world. The Commonwealth Glacier is a famous glacier in Antarctica. A glacier in Iceland actually surrounds an active volcano.

Malaspina Glacier in Alaska is the largest ice mass in North America. Other North American glaciers can be found in Montana and Canada. The biggest glacier in the world is Humboldt Glacier in Greenland.

The top of Mount Everest in Tibet is the highest point in the world. From there people can see three glaciers. They can see what nature has created with the forces of water and very cold temperatures.

Glaciers surround Mount Everest.

Chapter 3

The Power of Wind

One of nature's forces is invisible. It has no taste or smell. We can feel it, though. We can also see what it does. It makes a sailboat glide across a lake. It lifts a kite high in the sky. It's wind.

Wind is really just moving air. The faster it moves, the more we notice what it does. Wind can be a cool, gentle breeze on a hot day. It can bring clouds with rain for plants. In the middle of winter, the wind can be a freezing blast. Wind carries the weather of the seasons.

We cannot see wind, but we can see what it does.

Wind can be very powerful. A strong wind can stir up huge waves in the ocean. Together the forces of wind and water can easily sink large ships. In 1994 strong winds and high waves sank a huge boat off the coast of Finland in less than 20 minutes.

At certain times of the year, cool air moves in over an ocean. The cool air sends the warm, wet air upward. High winds and heavy rain can develop, then mighty storms we call hurricanes, cyclones, and typhoons. These fierce storms can take several days to reach land. Once they do, they can destroy whole cities.

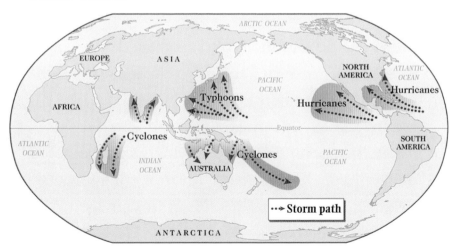

Hurricanes are known as cyclones and typhoons in other parts of the world.

Winds in hurricanes, cyclones, and typhoons move in a circle. In southern storms the winds blow clockwise. In northern storms the winds blow the other way.

The center of a hurricane's circular winds is called the eye of the storm. The eye is clear of rain, wind, and clouds. It is perfectly quiet. But winds outside the eye can reach a speed of 200 miles (320 kilometers) per hour.

Hurricanes, cyclones, and typhoons are really the same thing. What we call these storms depends on where they begin. Hurricanes start in the warm areas of the North Atlantic Ocean, the Gulf of Mexico, the Caribbean Sea, and the eastern Pacific Ocean. Typhoons form in the warm waters of the western Pacific Ocean. Most cyclones start near Australia and in the Indian Ocean.

Hurricanes, cyclones, and typhoons are very violent. They can cause many deaths and much damage. In 1992 Hurricane Andrew hit southern Florida. It did almost $20 billion in damage to the states of Florida and Louisiana. More than 50 people died. Thousands were left homeless.

In 1998 one of the worst hurricanes in history hit Central America. Hurricane Mitch destroyed cities and villages. Mitch killed thousands of people and left many more homeless. Help poured in from all over the world. Rebuilding lives and homes takes a long time, though—much longer than it takes wind and water to destroy them.

This photograph of Hurricane Mitch shows its eye in the center.

Tornadoes are the strongest windstorms. They are like hurricanes, cyclones, and typhoons, but they form over land. First a low, dark cloud forms in the sky. A twisting, funnel-shaped cloud then spins down toward the ground. The speed of the wind in the funnel cloud can reach more than 300 miles (480 kilometers) an hour. Because of their twisting movement, tornadoes are often called twisters.

Tornadoes usually happen in the spring and summer. Most of them move at less than 35 miles (56 kilometers) per hour and last less than an hour. They destroy almost everything in their path. The southern and midwestern United States are often called Tornado Alley. You can probably guess why. Many tornadoes hit those parts of the United States.

We may not believe all of the things that happen to Dorothy in *The Wizard of Oz*, but tornadoes can do some very strange things. A 1915 tornado in Kansas carried five horses from a barn. They were later found a short distance away, unhurt and still tied to a rail from the barn.

A Texas tornado

Tornadoes that form over lakes or oceans are called waterspouts. A waterspout's strong winds pull water into its funnel cloud. When the cloud breaks apart, the amount of water inside can crush a ship! The Bay of Bengal in the Indian Ocean is famous for its waterspouts.

Water in clouds often meets very cold temperatures. Then we get the snow that brings winter fun. Sometimes strong winds join the snow. Then a lovely snowfall turns into a **blizzard**!

Four things can change a snowfall into a blizzard. First, the wind blows at 35 miles (56 kilometers) per hour or more. Second, the temperature drops to about 10° F (-12° C) or below.

In a blizzard, the wind blows from the north.

Third, the blowing snow makes it nearly
impossible for people to see. In a very bad
blizzard, farmers can get lost walking from their
house to the barn. Last, the blowing snow must
last for at least 3 hours. One of the worst
blizzards in history happened in March 1888.
This blizzard covered the northeastern part of
the United States.

Chapter 4

Snowflakes and Grains of Sand

Have you ever felt snow on a hill give way beneath you? Have you ever climbed to the top of a ridge of sand and found yourself sliding down? You may know why your body moves downward. It's gravity. Gravity is the force that pulls things toward the center of the earth. It's the reason things fall down instead of up.

When snow builds up on a mountain, an **avalanche** can occur. An avalanche is a huge mass of snow that moves down a mountain. Three forces of nature create an avalanche. First, water and cold temperatures create snow. Then gravity pulls the snow downward.

This avalanche in New Zealand is just starting.

19

Avalanches happen when layers of snow do not stick together. Warmer temperatures can thaw lower layers of snow and cause an avalanche. An earthquake can cause the snow to slide, too. Sometimes the movement of an animal or person can start an avalanche. Even a loud noise is enough to send snow crashing down a slope.

Believe it or not, there are different kinds of avalanches. A dry snow avalanche occurs when a new snowfall is dry and powdery. The snow does not stick together. A wet snow avalanche happens when wet, heavy snow does not stick together. In a slab avalanche, a thick, wide slab of snow breaks away. It slides down a mountain like a board. Slab avalanches can travel up to 100 miles (160 kilometers) an hour. In 1983 a slab avalanche carried more than 1 billion pounds (454,000,000 kilograms) of snow down a mountain in Alaska.

Avalanches can happen wherever snow covers large mountains. During World War I, several avalanches crashed down the mountains of Italy. The sound of gunfire started these avalanches that buried about 18,000 soldiers.

An avalanche in Alaska

Scientists work hard to keep some avalanches from happening. They plant trees on mountains. The trees help keep the snow in one place. The scientists also use dynamite to keep snow from building up.

A **sand dune** is a sand hill shaped by the wind. Sand dunes form over long periods of time. Dunes are found in deserts and along oceans, rivers, and lakes. Sand travels on the wind until something, such as a tree or a rock, gets in the way. Then the sand falls to the ground. This goes on for many years until a dune forms.

Sand dunes grow and move. Grains of sand blow up the side of the dune that faces the wind. These grains fall over the top of the dune and land on the other side. This steep side of the dune is the **slipface**. When a layer of sand breaks away and slides down the slipface, the dune moves forward. Dunes can travel 60 to 80 feet (18 to 24 meters) each year.

The world's tallest dunes stand in the Sahara Desert. Some are 1525 feet (465 meters) high. The beauty of these sand dunes reminds us that nature's forces create as well as destroy.

Some sand dunes have one surprising feature. They make noise! This happens when the grains of sand move and rub against one another. Digging in or stomping on a dune can make it sing, squeak, or boom. Kelso Dune in California makes barking sounds. Sand Mountain in Nevada booms!

Wind is the force of nature that creates sand dunes.

Chapter 5

Shake, Rattle, and Roll

Snow can crash down a mountain slope. Sand dunes can creep along a lake shore. What about the earth itself? The ground beneath your feet may seem to be solid and unchanging. But down below the ground, the earth is in motion.

The earth's crust, or surface, is made of a layer of rock. This rock isn't in one piece, though. It's broken into several pieces called plates.

Scientists think that gravity causes the plates to move. The earth's plates are always moving. Usually they just slide past one another. When they smash into or pull away from each other, an earthquake occurs.

An earthquake can open up deep cracks in the ground.

The San Francisco Earthquake of 1906 caused many fires.

Most earthquakes begin at the edges of the plates. These edges, or **fault lines**, are large cracks in the earth's surface. The San Andreas Fault runs through California. Many powerful earthquakes have occurred along this fault, including the famous 1906 San Francisco earthquake.

When a strong earthquake occurs, shock waves spread out through the earth from the center of the quake. Bridges pull apart, dams crack and cause floods, and tall buildings crumble.

Damage created by a 1989
California earthquake

Scientists use the **Richter scale** to measure the strength of an earthquake's waves. The scale begins at 1.0. Earthquakes of 6.0 or more are the most dangerous.

Some Major Earthquakes Around the World

Year	Place	Richter Scale Rating
1905	Kangra, India	8.6
1906	San Francisco, California	8.3
1906	Valparaiso, Chile	8.6
1920	Gansu, China	8.6
1923	Yokohama, Japan	8.3
1927	Nan-Shan, China	8.3
1933	Japan	8.9
1946	Honshu, Japan	8.4
1960	Southern Chile	9.5
1964	Anchorage, Alaska	9.2

Sinkholes also occur because of movement under the ground. First, underground water slowly eats away rock. A large cave replaces the rock. Next, ground water fills the cave. Last, the land over the cave grows weaker and finally sinks.

In 1981 a large sinkhole opened up in Winter Park, Florida. A house, a shop, five cars, a pickup truck, part of the town's swimming pool, and many trees fell into the sinkhole. All of this happened within 24 hours!

The sinkhole in Winter Park, Florida

Quicksand often looks like a pool of water.

Water under the earth's surface can have a powerful effect. Sand is usually solid. People can walk on it. Cars can drive on it. But if water rises up through the sand, the water keeps the grains of sand apart. The sand is no longer solid. Instead, it is **quicksand**!

Quicksand cannot support weight. When people or animals try to walk on it, gravity pulls them under. The more they struggle, the faster they sink. Quicksand forms along oceans as well as on the shores and bottoms of rivers.

One famous patch of quicksand lies by a church on an island near France. Long ago it was difficult for people to travel to the island. After the fast-rising ocean tide went out, quicksand remained. A special road now makes traveling to the island easier. But tourists must be careful where they park their car!

The well-known patch of quicksand near France

Scientists ride in helicopters to study volcanoes.

The forces of heat and water can change the shape of the land in many ways. Volcanoes and hot springs are striking examples of these powerful forces. A volcano is an opening in the earth's crust. This opening is formed when hot gases and melted rock, or **magma**, burst through the crust. When magma reaches the earth's surface, it is called lava. When the lava hardens, mountains start to take shape.

Millions of years ago, volcanoes helped form the land on Earth. Most rocks on our planet started as lava and ash from volcanoes. Some volcanoes formed where the crust under oceans pulled apart. Iceland, Hawaii, and other islands were formed by underwater volcanoes.

Volcanoes create mountains and islands, but they can also destroy cities and towns. When a volcano **erupts**, lava, gas, ash, dust, and rocks shoot high into the air. They can cover land and water for miles around. Lava is red-hot as it hits the earth. Its temperature can reach over 2000° F (1,093° C). In A.D. 79, Italy's Mount Vesuvius erupted. Within a very short time, ash and lava buried the town of Pompeii and most of its people.

Island volcanoes can cause another disaster—tsunamis. After an island volcano erupts, it sometimes will fall inward. This fall makes the seafloor move. The sudden movement creates the deadly waves of a tsunami.

Volcanoes are dangerous, but they can help people and the environment. Within a few years after an eruption, ash becomes rich soil. **Pumice** is a lightweight rock that comes from lava. We use pumice to grind and polish metal.

The magma that creates volcanoes also warms underground water to create hot springs. Some of these springs are flowing streams of hot water. Others are calm or bubbling pools.

The eruption of a volcano in Hawaii

Many hot springs are found in areas where volcanoes have erupted. Water from rain and snow seeps underground. It reaches the magma and heats up. Then the hot water rises up through the rock. When the water breaks through the earth's surface, a hot spring is formed.

Each year thousands of people visit hot springs around the world. The warmth of the water eases sore muscles. The temperature of hot springs is often more than 140° F (60° C). Minerals in the springs make the water colorful.

A hot spring in the United States' Yellowstone National Park

Geysers are often found near hot springs. A geyser is a spring that shoots steam and hot water into the air. It begins to form when water seeps deep below the surface of the earth. The water is heated by magma and becomes steam. As the steam rises, it lifts water toward the earth's surface. Suddenly the steam bursts through an opening in the ground. It pushes the water up with great force, sometimes hundreds of feet into the air.

Strokkur, a famous geyser in Iceland, shoots steam and hot water up to 66 feet (20 meters) in the air.

Some geysers erupt regularly every few minutes or hours. Others do not spout off for weeks or months.

Chapter 6

Exploring Nature's Power

Every year millions of people visit places to see what Earth's forces can do. They learn how glaciers and volcanoes are formed. They watch a geyser erupting or bathe in a hot spring. Some people might even hear a sand dune boom. Many countries have set up national parks to preserve the earth's natural wonders.

Glacier National Park is the home of many glaciers.

Glacier National Park in North America has almost 50 glaciers. Grinnell Glacier is the largest and covers 298 acres (119 hectares).

The Sahara Desert in Africa has more sand dunes than anywhere else in the world. Few people visit these dunes. The Sahara is too hot. Dunes in the United States are easier to reach. Oregon Dunes National Recreation Area lies along the Pacific Ocean. These dunes rise up to 500 feet (152 meters) above sea level.

The tallest dunes in the United States are in the Great Sand Dunes National Monument. These Colorado dunes are almost 800 feet (244 meters) high. A park along Lake Michigan has some of the world's largest lake shore dunes.

Mauna Loa in Hawaii is the world's largest active volcano. Nearby is Kilauea Crater. Both of these volcanoes can be found in Hawaii Volcanoes National Park. Visitors to Italy can see Mount Etna, the tallest active volcano in Europe. It last erupted in 1998.

The world's most famous geysers are in the United States, Iceland, and New Zealand.

Yellowstone National Park has more than 200 geysers, including the famous Steamboat Geyser and Old Faithful. Iceland's biggest geyser is Strokkur, which means "the churner." New Zealand's best-known geysers are Pohutu and Wairoa.

Try to visit some natural wonders near you. See what nature's power can do!

Each year thousands of people come to see Old Faithful in Yellowstone National Park.

GLOSSARY

avalanche a large mass of snow that moves down a mountain

blizzard a strong windstorm with much snow

erupt to burst out

fault line a crack in the earth's surface

geyser a spring or other underground source of water that shoots steam and hot water into the air

glacier a slow-moving mass of ice and snow

magma melted rock inside the earth

pumice a lightweight rock that comes from lava

quicksand sand mixed with water into which heavy objects sink easily

Richter scale the scale scientists use to measure the strength of earthquake waves

sand dune a large hill of sand shaped by wind

sinkhole a hole carved by underground water

slipface the side of a sand dune facing away from the wind

tsunami a group of ocean waves caused by an earthquake or a volcano

Index

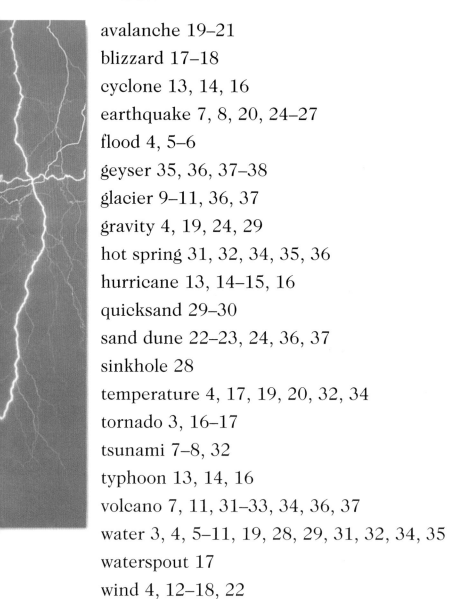